Adventures of the Cabin Kids:
88 Mountain View Cir.

By
Zachary Lipscomb

Copyright © 2019 by Zachary Lipscomb
All rights reserved. No part of this book may be reproduced, scanned,
or distributed in any printed or electronic form without permission.
First Edition: july 2019
Printed in the United States of America
ISBN: 1645502872
ISBN: 9781645502876

Any people depicted in stock imagery provided by Thinkstock are models,
and such images are being used for illustrative purposes only.
Certain stock imagery © Thinkstock

Because of the dynamic nature of the Internet, any web addresses or links contained in this book may have changed since publication and may no longer be valid. The views expressed in this work are solely those of the author and do not necessarily reflect the views of the publisher, and the publisher hereby disclaims any responsibility for them

Little Bud

"Our Cabin"

Hi, they call me Little Bud, I am second in command of the Cabin Kids. Along with my glasses, hiking boots, and baseball cap, the best part of my outfit is my BB gun. Okay I'm just kidding, I am all too young to carry a BB gun, it is a toy BB gun with a cork in it. I carry this for protection, you know in case I see a bear or something. I am the younger brother of Pj, he is our leader, Pj is the lucky one, yes he gets to carry a bow and arrow, no animal or anything in our path stands a chance against him. He is very tough in his backwards cap and unbuttoned flannel, with his blue jeans and hiking boots. Oh yes, I almost forgot our pal Sunshine, she is not very scary. Sunshine stands about 3 and a half feet tall with blonde curls, and her overalls cover her yellow plaid shirt, and she carries a magnifying glass in her pocket. After a long car ride our last stop lead to this place we have never been before, this beautiful log cabin on this mountain with a really big lake in the back yard. As we walked along the porch that went all the way from the front, around the side to the back, we passed this old hand made wooden sign we could not read. Of course as brave as Pj is he walked up and brushed away the cobwebs to find a little wooden

Grandma

railroad with the words "The Other Side of the Tracks". Right away little Sunshine got excited "Pj, Little Bud, are we going to see a train?" she asked, so I looked to Pj for the answer. After a little pause and a fix of his cap, he looked down at us and said "guys I have a good feeling about this place." As we ventured past the sign we came to a break in the railing that opened up to a platform for some stairs. But these were such cool stairs, spaced out perfectly around the whole railing were big wooden cowboy boots. We continued around to the door, where we passed a porch swing and some rocking chairs, as we strolled through the door our attention is grabbed by the deer heads on the walls. Suddenly this felt like a scary place until our sweet Grandma, standing there in her long sleeve plaid shirt and blue jeans, pushed up her glasses and said "welcome to Our Cabin."

"Down the Tracks"

    As we finished up supper, we were so excited to see what this place had in store for us. Sunshine ate so fast she had a belly ache. "Sunshine you cannot go out for 1 hour, you need time for your tummy to settle." said Grandma. But Pj looked at us with a big smile and whispered

    "while grandma cleans up from dinner we can sneak out the front door." Sure enough PJ held open the screen door while we burst through with excitement. Catching us on the other side was the railing, as we looked over into the yard there was an old tree with a handmade green swing on it. That was Papa Lippy's surprise for us, he is a tall man with dark jeans, boots, and a red shirt, as he stood there by the shed down stairs with his blue hat and dark red beard, he watched us race by to see who can get to the swing first. He yelled out "don't go near the tracks." "But Papa I want to see a train!" said Sunshine as Pj and I nodded our heads to agree. "You all are too young to be playing by the tracks, have I made myself clear?" bellowed Papa. An hour went by as we took turns pushing each other on the swing, waiting for a moment to venture to the tracks, when out of the woods came a noise of brush and twigs breaking under feet. Sunshine jumped off of the swing to hide behind me, "Pj, what was that?" she asked. Pj strung his arrow and began to draw back the string, only to see a beautiful momma deer prancing onto the tracks with her baby clumsily following. We couldn't resist, as we followed down the stairs taking us from the yard to the tracks, we saw the baby deer struggling to run down the tracks eventually stumbling to the ground. Pj raced to the baby deer only to find that it's hoof was stuck between the spike and the rail of the track. "We have to get him to his mother" said Sunshine, "what if it gets dark and she never finds him?" she asked. I asked Pj "what about the tracks you heard what papa said," he answered sternly, "we have to save this deer, I'm sure Papa will understand!" After several minutes we were able to set the deer free and he pranced off into the fog. Of course as we realized we were pretty far down the tracks Pj decided we should keep going to make sure the deer made it to his mother. Pj lead us down the tracks through the thick fog, on the right there seemed to be an opening in the woods, as we inched closer not knowing what to expect being that our vision was limited. "Look, look over there!" said Sunshine, off in the distance we could see two dark shadows trotting through the fog, all we could see were their hooves meeting the brown grass of what appeared to be a deer field. We continued down the tracks rounding the curve bringing us to a different part of the field, it was separated by a creek running through the middle making it look like two fields. While the front part was flat and grazed, the back had what looked like a road going up further into the woods with an old house at the top. We came to a bridge that crossed over the same creek that split the deer field, at the end of the bridge was a steep slope down to the grass. "Stop! over there, in the woods, what is that red thing?' Pj asked. He slid down the gravel, darted into the trees, and as he pulled back the branches to get closer, a tire rolled out and landed in the creek. "What is it Pj?" asked Sunshine. "It's a car, a red car," he explained.

"The Red Car"

"It seems to be a wreck." As Sunshine ran down with her spyglass, I ran to get the tire before it floated away. I got the tire to shore and yelled out "Pj see if there is anything in the trunk?" Pj opened the glove box to see two rats come running out, "whoa! you scared me little rats," Pj exclaimed. I began walking into the thicket to help Pj and Sunshine investigate. Where I accidentally bumped into this wooden pole sticking out of the ground in the opening of the thicket. Without warning a boobie trap was set off and Sunshine was wrapped in a net, not able to escape. "Help Help! Pj Little Bud I've been trapped." yelled Sunshine. So I ran over to cut her free with my pocket knife, before Pj could get over to help he was tripped by a wire triggering a

bell to ring. "Guys get down be quiet someone is obviously watching this place" whispered Pj. After what seemed like an hour of staring into the woods, where that road lead in the back of the deer field, we stood up to continue our investigation. I moved to the trunk of the car prying on it with a board I found in the creek, "Pj can you give me a hand opening this trunk?" I asked. We pried and pried, finally with our feet on the bumper for leverage it sprung loose sending Pj and I into the air landing in a pile of brush. "Oh my, are you guys okay?" asked Sunshine. I sprung to my feet and ran to the trunk to see what I could find, "Whoa, guys check this out" I whispered excitedly. "Wow it's a hatchet, Little Bud I want you to have this." said Pj "For your bravery and fast rescue of Sunshine from that trap, I think you've earned it" He explained. With shaking hands and broken voice, I thanked him. I stored my new hatchet in the back of my jeans, we continued our search of the trunk to see if we could find any kind of clue as to who this car once belonged to. Pj pulled out some rope and a lantern, "Sunshine I want you to have this, to keep us safe from the dark." said Pj. As he tied it around her waist using the rope as a belt, we heard rustling in the distance, "Pj look over there." I yelled. Running down the road were three boys head to toe in black, with ripped jeans and t-shirts with holes in them. One had red hair the other two had dark straight hair. The redhead seemed to be the leader because he was carrying a handmade weapon, made out of two rocks tied together strung to a stick. Pj gathered us behind him with his bow drawn, he aimed for the leader as they continued through the field while swinging his rocks overhead. We were somewhat hidden in the brush, but they could still see us. They started getting closer, "Pj are they going to hurt us?" asked Sunshine, in a scared voice. I stepped up beside Pj grabbing my hatchet from my jeans, and before he could answer I nervously responded "we got this." As they grew closer the leader yelled out "we are the Field Boys, leave now or else." "This doesn't sound good guys, be ready." Said Pj

"Chase is on"

The closer the Field Boys got the more scared poor Sunshine was, "um Pj, Little Bud I don't think they are nice boys, I think we should go" said Sunshine. Before they could reach us Pj ordered us to run, he grabbed the rest of the rope and I stuffed everything into the bag we found in the trunk of the car. "After them, don't let them get away!" exclaimed the leader of the Field Boys. Pj lead us through the deer field dodging the rocks and sticks that were being thrown at us. Whoever these boys were they really did not want us in this field. After a few minutes of running I noticed that we were still on the other side of the creek, luckily in the middle of the field we found an opening in the brush exposing the creek. "This is our chance to cross here guys" yelled Pj, "but I can't swim" Sunshine replied. "It shouldn't be but waist deep" I said, " He's right Sunshine, even if you have a hard time getting across we will be on either side of you" Said Pj. We came to a stop at the edge of the creek gazing upon it seemed so wide and almost impossible to cross, but we had no choice. We looked at each other, locked hands and splash! Treading through the water I looked back and the Field Boys were nowhere to be found, "Pj we lost them" I yelled out, "good let's get across and we'll be okay" he said. Pj had already made it to the other side not knowing that Sunshine and I were stuck in the mud, the current was too strong. "Help! help! it's too strong Pj" I tied the rope around Sunshine and I and threw the other end to Pj. After a few tries he caught it, "I got it, now as I pull, you guys need to try and swim towards me. We can do this together" said Pj. As soon as we picked up our feet and began to swim it got worse. The current just carried us away, but Pj is a wise leader, he had the rope wrapped around the tree using it for leverage. Finally, we made it to shore, as we lie there in the hay catching our breath we hear a yelling in the distance, "Oh the creek couldn't do the trick, looks like we can finish

them off ourselves boys!" Yelled the leader. "Oh no! how did they find us?" asked Sunshine, "there must be another way across this creek." said Pj. "Look up there a ways, there is some more brush, we can hide out in there" I pointed out. So we darted across the field into the brush tripping over what felt like barbed wire, "Ouch! what is this stuff?" I asked "It must be a briar patch I've heard Papa talk about these" said Sunshine. Struggling through the brush for a while we came out on the other side cut from head to toe, little thin paper cuts. "Let's hide out here for a minute and see if they are really gone this time" said Pj. We patiently waited and waited and waited, no sooner did we turn around, "You can't hide long form us, this is our field." said the leader. The only thing separating us from them was a little stream of water, we were at a standoff. "We are the Cabin Kids we mean you no harm" said Pj, "I am Mcgillicutty, leader of the Field Boys, these are my brothers Scooter and Mattman, you are on our land we will do anything to keep you off." Scooter was the smallest of the three with a dark brown bowl cut, while Mattman was the skinnier of the boys. They jumped the stream and the chase was on again. "Guys over there, what is that?" Sunshine asked, there was a building, as we approached it we noticed it was vacant. "we can hide out here good eye Sunshine." said Pj. When we got to the door, Pj gave the knob a wiggle, and of course it was locked. "Little Bud try the window." He ordered, as I pried it opened with ease, we climbed inside and locked the whole place down. Inside there were tables, chairs, and benches with a podium. "Do you think they do weddings here Pj" I asked, "or maybe it's some kind of church" suggested Sunshine. "Whatever it is we are staying safe in here for now" said Pj. We ventured into the kitchen for hiding. It was the only place where we were completely hidden, as the whole building was windows. The windows on one side overlooked a little water hole, on the other side they overlooked the lake that leads to Our Cabin. "We need to plan an escape." uttered Pj, "Look I see some bridges leading to that island we can see from our back yard" I suggested. There were three bridges leading to the island and the only one close to us, without the Field Boys seeing us, was a rotten white one. We waited a while and made a run for the bridge, crossing a parking lot basketball court. But running out of the field of grass, came Mcgillicutty, "there they are boys, let's go." We sprinted on to the bridge that crumbled under our feet and into the lake. Just when we thought we were safe, we saw the other two bridges were perfectly fine, allowing the Field Boys to meet us in the middle. "We will fight for this island" said Mcgillicutty.

"Battle for the Island"

"You want a battle you got it," answered Pj. As we looked around with our backs touching, there were targets everywhere. "What is this?" asked Sunshine. "This my friends, is our playground," said Mcgillicutty. "If you can win more island games than us, you go free." I took another gaze there were two free standing targets for a bow, but it was the two other targets painted on a tree I could not figure out. "Pj what are those for?" I asked. "Hatchets Little Bud, hatchets" he answered nervously, "That's what I was afraid of." I stated. I knew Pj had the bow and arrow challenge won, but I have never thrown a hatchet before. In fact, I just got my first hatchet when we found it in the car. What was I going to do, I don't have any way to practice? "What is my game?" asked Sunshine. "Do you see those cans over there?" Mcgillicutty asked. The three of us looked over and gulped. "BB gun shoot out!" "You got it girl." said Mcgillicutty "You'll be facing Scooter" said Pj "So you got this, and Little Bud you can take on Mattman in the hatchets." "You guys we can do this, if we beat these guys we are free to go wherever we want on the mountain, whenever we want." Pj confidently whispered. "The rules of the games are as follows" said Mcgillicutty. "The Bow Show: you get three shots, the highest score wins.

Bullseye is 10 points, yellow ring is 5 points, blue ring is 1 point. The Hatchet Throw: you get three throws; the points are the same as The Bow Show. The BB Gun Shoot Out: you see the five cans; they are worth 2 points each. If the can doesn't fall off the plank it does not count. Have I been clear?" "Who goes first?" I asked. "The Field Boys will go first in every event." said Mcgillicutty. Pj called for a huddle to game plan, we didn't really know what we were going to do, Pj was the only one experienced in his game. Sunshine and I nervously watched on, as Mcgillicutty began to draw his first arrow back, he hit high right on the blue ring and Pj couldn't help but smile. He drew back arrow number two, "Bullseye" he yelled out, he rapidly drew back arrow number three as if he did not want to lose his groove. "Bullseye again," he said. Pj walked up, as brave as ever" 21, I can beat that" he said, and like a machine gun he landed two bullseyes with the first two arrows. He settled down wiped his sweat from his forehead and looked at Sunshine and I, he focused back on the target and reached over his shoulder for his arrow. "I can't watch" cried Sunshine, and we both covered our eyes, and then the whistling of the arrow cutting through the air came to an abrupt stop. We looked over and Pj was jumping in the air, he yelled "25, I got 25 guys." "Okay so that is one for the Cabin Kids" said Sunshine. Mcgillicutty fell to his knees in defeat, as I walked to the next game with my shaking knees and pale as a ghost. "Mattman if you lose this your swimming back to shore" ordered Mcgillicutty. "Little Bud focus let the head of the hatchet guide the way," said Pj. I patiently awaited while Mattman threw his first hatchet, I hear a thud and look at the tree, "it's blue, yes!" I whispered to myself. "Boy you better step it up" said Mcgillicutty. He threw his second hatchet and hit the yellow, so he now has 6 points, so of course I start to think he is zoning in on the bullseye. He backs away from the line to take a breath and regroup, at the same time I walk up to the line to get a feel for it and it felt like a mile. He stepped up and released, Pj ran to the tree because the hatchet was right on the line between the yellow and blue. "What is it?" I asked "It's blue, it's blue" Pj exclaimed. Mcgillicutty ran up to be sure, he walked back with his head down in defeat. "Little Bud, now all you have to do is hit one bullseye, and you win with one hatchet" whispered Sunshine. I step up to the line and take a deep breath, I look over at Pj and then at Mcgillicutty. As I hold up the hatchet and aim it at the tree, I can't focus in because of how shaky I am, I pull back and release. As soon as the hatchet left my hand I covered my eyes I couldn't watch, no way no how. Next thing I know Pj tackles me with excitement. "Bullseye, bullseye, Little Bud you did it, you win 10 to 7" Pj yelled out. "We win!" yelled Sunshine. "Wait, does this mean I don't have to do the shoot out?" she asked. "That's right Sunshine" answered Pj. The Field Boys walked over the bridge in defeat.

"Rescue Mission"

Pj, Sunshine, and I were still basking in glory after our victory over the Field Boys, then we realized we had no idea how to get back to our Cabin. We looked around and saw two bridges, one that leads to another island, and one that leads to the other side of the lake, taking us further from home. "That way will take us further from home right Pj?" asked Sunshine. "Yes, but it seems to be the safest route, there are a lot of cabins we will pass, and it is getting a little late." he said. Pj was right, the sun had fallen just below the mountain top, but not quite set yet. So we probably only have two hours of daylight left. "I just wish we had a way to get one of our boats." said Sunshine. Directly across from the island we were standing on, we could see our back yard. Right by the lake we have a paddle boat and a rowboat, none of which we could get to. We headed toward the other side of the lake, walking over a red bridge that had a gate on it. "Oh

great now we are stranded." uttered Sunshine. "She is right Pj, what are we going to do?" I asked. Pj removed his cap and ran his fingers through his hair, almost like he was admitting defeat. I knew that if Pj felt this way that we were not in good shape. He paced and paced scratching his head, as he placed his cap back on his head, he answered "we swim." "But Pj we have no idea what is in the lake." said Sunshine "Yeah there could be snakes, or even snapping turtles." I added. We let the idea ponder for a few more minutes. Just as I was walking to the edge to put my feet in, I hear a voice. "Cabin Kids to the rescue!" "Who is that Little Bud?" asked Pj. "Look its K-bug and Molly" I answered. K-bug and Molly are the youngest members of the Cabin Kids, they always match with their pink shirts under overalls and pigtails, except Molly has brown hair while K-bug has blonde curls. As we boarded the rowboat and Pj pushed off the island, it started raining rocks. "Get down, it's the Field Boys again" I yelled.

"Sore losers"

"Who are the Field Boys?" asked K-bug. While Pj took over the rowing, he explained "the Field Boys are very mean kids K-bug." "Yeah they challenged us to a series of games and told us if we won we were free to roam the mountain." Sunshine added. "Well did you guys win?" asked Molly. "Yes, fair and square." I answered. "They must be sore losers." said K-bug. K-bug was right that was the only good explanation as to why these boys would be after us again. So the five of us were stranded in the middle of the lake with this row boat, we had no idea where to get off. I can see our cabin from where we were, but the only dock on our side of the lake was half under water. "Pj that dock is the only way." I suggested. "Guys get ready to get wet." Pj replied. Pj turned the boat around and headed for the dock, and as I looked across the lake I could see Mcgillicutty leading his boys around to try and meet us there. "Um Pj, you better row faster they are coming." I yelled. As we grew closer you could see the ripples in the lake from every rock they threw, and with the few they got to us left dents in the boat. "Little Bud, grab the rope and try to lasso the dock." Pj ordered. After two tries I finally got it, "great now pull us in." said Molly. Finally, we made landfall, and just as Pj was the last one to get off, I could see Mcgillicutty rounding the lake. To our left was a black berry patch that arched over the path of grass, we met them in the opening. "We meet again." said Mcgillicutty. "We meet again." Pj replied angrily.

"Round Two"

"I see your tribe has grown Pj." said Mcgillicutty. As Pj and Mcgillicutty were in a standoff, I noticed a set of stairs to our right, leading directly to the tracks. So I slowly lead the girls up while Pj tried to reason with the Field Boys. "Mcgillicutty we won fair and square, we are free to do as we wish." said Pj sternly. "You did win and I did say that, but this is still our mountain, and I don't like you here." he replied. "Pj let's go!" I yelled. He ran up the gravel, skipping the steps, and again we were on the run. "You were right Pj they are mean boys, what is wrong with them?" Molly asked. "I was wondering the same thing this isn't their mountain, how do you own a mountain?" asked K-bug. As we ran down the tracks again, Sunshine noticed we were running the opposite way of our cabin. "Um Pj shouldn't we be going that way?" "I don't want them to know where we live, I don't want them to destroy any of our stuff." Answered Pj "So we need to lose them again before we go anywhere near home?" asked Molly. "Yes." Pj answered. We got

further away and just as I looked back K-bug had fell and skinned her knee on the tracks. "Pj wait up, K-bug fell." I yelled out. "K-bug, what did I tell you about running with your shoes untied?" Asked Pj. A while later she got back to her feet, after wrapping her knee and double knotting her shoe so this wouldn't happen again. "Can we stop running now Pj, I think we lost them." said Molly. While walking down the tracks we came to the road, and looked around to figure out which way we should go. "Guys I think we should stay on the tracks, this way we don't get lost." I suggested. "That is a good idea, we do not know the mountain yet." added Sunshine. "We will stay on the tracks and continue but not much further it is getting dark and I don't want to be out here while the bears play." answered Pj. "Bears, are you sure there are bears out here?" Molly asked nervously. "Of course there are bears it's all woods out here." I answered. As we passed the road we couldn't help but keep going. Several yards down the track there was a white sign with a "W" on it. The closer we got we could tell there was an opening in the brush, like some sort of trail. "What is in there?" asked Sunshine "I don't know but I am ready to find out." said Pj. "Shh, Shh, guys listen, I hear water" whispered Molly. So we headed down the tracks towards the trail opening, sliding down the rocks landing in the clay, Pj stopped us all at the bottom. "Stay close guys" ordered Pj. Ding, ding ding ding, "oh man that's our warning bell." said K-bug. "Yup Grandma wants us home, if we hurry maybe we can hunt for lightning bugs." added Molly. "But I really want to follow this trail." said Sunshine. At the same time Pj and I answered, "there's always tomorrow girls, there's always tomorrow."

88 Mountain View Cir. Is the actual address of the magical place, my family and I, called Our Cabin for so many years. Everyone should have a place like this of their own in life. A place with no worry in the world. My intention with this book is to share with the world exactly what took place, on the "OTHER SIDE OF THE TRACKS

www.ingramcontent.com/pod-product-compliance
Lightning Source LLC
Chambersburg PA
CBHW041122070526
44584CB00002B/250